Presented to:

_____

From:

_____

Date:

_____

©2022 Jasmine Be, Power 2 Tread, LLC

ISBN 978-0-578-29694-4

Published by Power 2 Tread, LLC, P.O. Box 7391, Greensboro, NC 27417

Printed in the United States of America.

Write As I Tell You, Precious Daughter

LUKE 10:19

To You, From God, Through Me

Hello Precious Sibling,

Thank you for taking the time, the funds and the effort to purchase this book. It contains messages from our Father to us. I received these messages during my personal times of prayer, worship and soaking with Him. Initially, they seemed specifically for me, but after a while I thought to myself "I don't think He's just talking to me anymore." LOL

Sure enough, months later, the Holy Spirit directed me to gather the messages and publish them for **us all** to view and hold fast to. Read them in the order listed or skip around as led.

May this book encourage you, sharpen your gifts and catapult you into the destiny which God has for you. In Jesus name, Amen.

Jasmine Be

Woman, Like You

I had a vision of the woman with the issue of blood. She had no help, no support. People knew she was there on the ground, but did not help her get to Jesus. The spirits of inferiority & rejection were upon her. She lacked help, even from the Apostles, who saw her below. Many stepped on her. She was accustomed to low treatment, which is exactly why she did not stop reaching. "Like you", said the Lord to me.

Read the account in each gospel.

The Blessing Of The Lord

Write as I tell you, Precious Daughter. The Spirit of the Lord, indeed, the Blessing of the Lord is <u>still</u> upon you. Nothing has gone wrong, you have not gone astray. Transitioning is happening within you. Be not dismayed at the lack of social media consistency & content. Be not concerned about the lack & loss of followers. The power, authority & conviction which <u>I</u> have put in you causes others to flee. Be not concerned, be not dismayed. I will surely elevate you at the appointed time(s).

Busyness ≠ Your Worth

The heaviness you feel is emptiness; of family time, of love you feel is missing, of responsibility, of worth. You've associated busyness with worth for so long that you think it equates, but it does not, My Daughter. Rest. In. It. Do not concern yourself with how others perceive your break. It, in itself is revolutionary; to show leaders that breaks are okay & necessary. Because when I elevate you, ALL will know & understand this current silence. So. Rest. Don't rush to return. The time is not yet. RE-GROUP.

At Peace In The Wait

Complete the assignments from this past week. Cast down thoughts that I did not give you. Be at peace. Rest. Assured that I've got you. Nothing missing. Nothing lacking. I am not upset with you, you are taking on too much. Wait for Me, for My direction. Wait. Be at peace in the wait. Frustration leave in the name of Jesus. Take deep breaths of My air into your lungs. Prepare for your new life with the excitement. It is coming & is here now, says the Lord. In Jesus name, Amen.

You Are A Light Source

Write as I tell you, My Beautiful Daughter. I indeed saw you. Saw you among the lattice. The lace & the veil. Never forget that it is I who am the first & the Original Creator, which makes Me the Creative. Think of the beautiful birds that I have created. Think of the skies as the light source changes. Think of the light sources & their obedience unto Me. Be like them in your obedience unto Me.

Do your job no matter the storm, no matter the season. Play your role in the earth. Though many may forget your presence; take it for granted, they would surely notice your absence. So keep showing up because you are needed. You are where I, the He Almighty have placed you. A permanent fixture. A permanent position. Serving many purposes. Useful in many ways. People explore & find out, seek out more reasons as to why I made you. They have yet to discover them all & they never will. Amen♡

Day Of Multiplication

Write as I tell you, My Precious One. The Lord bless you & keep you. I make My face to shine upon YOU! Never forget that.

This is the day the Lord has made. Rejoice & be glad in it. #gladness on THIS DAY. Day of multiplication for all to see & know that I am God, that I am the Lord YOUR God who goes with you & fights every battle. None can withstand you because none can withstand Me, says the Lord of HOSTS. It is I who go before you & fight every battle. For the victory is already won, My Sweet Daughter. Sweet Daughter of Mine.♡

Continue

Continue to go forth & SHINE. Shine as I have called you to, SHINE with the Light I have placed upon you. Called to light up every dark space; the dark areas of your life & of those in your life. No corner will be left dim, no shadow around. Only the LIGHT. Amen♡

Discover And Uncover

On this day, My Daughter, you will discover & uncover many things. Governmental things, unearthen things, unusual things. Be prepared. For New Life.

Conspiracy

UFO

Supernatural

Don't be afraid of what I am to show you. For nothing can harm you. These are deep mysteries which others are afraid of, but not you. I will show you. You will uncover much discovery today. Think it not strange & fear not. For I am with you.

Let The World Know!

You have indeed heard from ME, My Daughter. Let the world know what I am doing through you. It's okay. No harm or disaster will come nigh you. Do as I say. You will be fine! In Jesus name. Amen!

All Is Well

Hello Daughter of Mine. You have done as I have asked of you. You indeed hear Me & obey. Think not on the former things, they are of old. You are where you are supposed to be; doing as I have asked of you.

Go forth and do. And Be. All is fine & will work as I have set it to accomplish. Think of ALL; what does it mean? ALL means everything. All encompassing. Even the things & scenarios you do not think of, those too are well. Do the assignments I give you & forget the old. Amen♡ With love!

His Fire

Fire, fire, fire

Fire down in my soul

Fire, fire, fire

The blaze is out of control

That is, my control

Because it's not mine

But His.

His anointing. His fire. His power.

Which flows through me

Flowing fire

Like a river

Down within me, bursting out of me

Leaping out as my spirit leaps up

Upward. Onward. Outward.

Forward March.

March forward. Amen

Splash, Splatter, Shine

Splash, splatter, shine. As you have your hands in position to receive, near your face, favor & grace splash & splatter onto the sides of your face. This causes your face to glow of My Glory. Let your light so shine among men. Be afraid not. Me intimidated not. Be not weary. For I am with you EVERYWHERE you go. You have been awarded ME! No place, no assignment is too hard for you because it is I Who Do It! Never forget to give ME the glory. Always! Though it <u>SHINES</u> on you, it came from & belongs to ME. In Jesus name, Amen.♡

All Of Me

Where I am taking you, you need all of ME; as much as you can get. So I stretch you, I press you, I advise what should be cleansed out of you to make way for ME. Detox with the Himalayan salt. It is I who created it & you for such a time as this.

Diving Into His Presence

While watching *Diving Into His Presence – Soaking In His Presence Instrumental* (YouTube). I do not own the rights to the video or any song mentioned.

Look at the waters of the video. It represents ME hovering over the deep. It represents I, going with you & being before you & surrounding you & watching over you in the sky. The clouds are ME. The wind is My breath.

🎵This is the air I breathe. Your Holy presence. Living in me. 🎵

The waves represent My Favor towards you. Splash, splatter, shining in the Son. There are blue shades in the sky which represent calmness. The Son is glowing through with a warm, knowing embrace. ♡Amen

The Example Of Jesus

Think of Jesus: Meekness to enter the earth at the time period He did – without technology & luxuries. He was calm because He knew & still knows WHO HE IS. Jesus didn't bother screaming at those who misunderstood, didn't over explain. Confident. Focused. Immovable! Amen. The crowd went from outrage & backing Him towards a cliff, to Him simply walking through the crowd. He didn't have to argue nor did He! Take it or leave it. Period! This IS the Word of the Lord. Good day & peace be unto you. Amen.

Reassurance

My Beloved, write as I tell you. I indeed love you. More than you know. I need you. To do My will, but also to be with Me, in Heaven. You are mine. No harm or disaster will ever come nigh you again. This is the PROMISE I have made to you. Stop upsetting yourself. All is well, as I have spoken numerous times. You want to be avenged, to retaliate, to cause sufferings, but vengeance is MINE. I Will Repay, says the Lord. Continue to do My will, stay on course. I will give you a sign. There is purpose in this. I have not forgotten you. Be patient. Fret not. In Jesus name, Amen. All had purpose, you won't remember the pain. Stay in My army, on My side. Amen. ♡

SHINE!

ontinue to go forth & <u>SHINE</u>. SHINE like never before, no matter what it looks like. SHINE! People used to get upset when I smiled, when I was happy so I would hide it, but <u>NO MORE</u>. This joy that I have the world didn't give it, the world can't take it away.

Through, Through, Through!

Through the trials, through the pain, through the rain. God is there! He is here! He is where I go & where I was! He is everlasting just as His love for us. He goes from everlasting to everlasting. <u>Throughout</u> all ages. World without end. Amen

Irreplaceable

Write as I tell you, My Precious, Irreplaceable Daughter. You are indeed irreplaceable. No one can compare to you in the earth. You do as I say, no matter the cost & I appreciate <u>you</u> for this! You shall surely live & not die, you shall live & declare My works! All of your days. Without recourse, without recompense.

For I know the plans I have for you says the Lord. Plans to prosper & not to harm you. To give you a <u>successful</u> HOPE AND FUTURE! Your use of "ands" comes from ME. I don't like to provide one thing but more than one; an abundance. One is not enough in most cases. With spouses, it is! You shall do My will & abide in ME ALL of your days & in every way. Goodbye to the writing for now, though I am with you ALWAYS! Amen

Connect with Jasmine!

linktr.ee/JasmineBe

She has another book; an intercessory prayer devotional!

Intercession 101: A Mom's Aid In Obedience

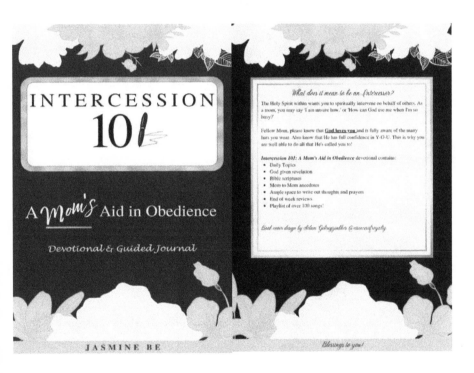

Available on Amazon.com and other retailers!

CPSIA information can be obtained
at www.ICGtesting.com
Printed in the USA
BVHW041535230622
640497BV00003BA/499